Body and Soul

New and Selected Poems

Body and Soul

New and Selected Poems

John Livingstone Clark

TORONTO

Exile Editions

2002

Copyright © EXILE EDITIONS LIMITED 2002
Copyright © JOHN LIVINGSTONE CLARK 2002

All rights reserved. The use of any part of this publication, reproduced, transmitted in any form or by any means, electronic, mechanical, photocopying, recording or otherwise stored in a retrieval system, without the prior consent of the publisher is an infringement of the copyright law.

This edition is published by Exile Editions Limited,
20 Dale Avenue, Toronto, Ontario, Canada M4W 1K4

Sales Distribution:
McArthur & Company
c/o Harper Collins
1995 Markham Road
Toronto, ON
M1B 5M8
toll free:
1 800 387 0117
(fax) 1 800 668 5788

Design by *Tim Hanna*

Cover Design by *Zero Weather*

Typeset at *Moons of Jupiter Inc.*

Final Formatting by *Michael Callaghan*

Author Photo by *Debbie Clark*

Printed and Bound at *Transcontinental Printing*

The publisher wishes to acknowledge the assistance toward publication of the Canada Council and the Ontario Arts Council.

ISBN 1-55096-562-X
Printed in Canada

to Krista, Brennan, & Gavin

off / sprung rhythms
with love
a given

Contents

Part III
The Art Catalogue

Part IV
The Ghost Father

Part IV
Stream Under Flight

Part VI
New Poems

Prologue: For Gavin, My Son

your mother screams downstairs to where I'm
just waking up
and I think, this is no ordinary squall
this is no bawling woman tired
of picking up books,
toys, the flotsam and jetsam
of a shaky alliance

this keening woman whose life is coming apart

and I tear up the stairs
as she tears the morning stillness
with her grief

and there you are, my precious boy, my only other
love   thrashing in your piss-soaked sheets
rigid
where once you were soft
ferocious
where once you were gentle
absent
where once your presence dazzled our lives

and I crouch and shake in fear
falling to my knees beside your wet-stained manger
crying, Why him, Lord? Why bend this beautiful light?

and carrying you downstairs wrapped in white
woollen blankets
I lay you on your side
lie beside you in the enveloping dark
your writhing, twisted form
a small cross in the storm

praying, Please Lord God, put the fire on me!
Put the lightning in my brain!
crying, Baby, baby, baby, baby, baby . . .
all out of my mind
though this is not ecstasy
this is the opposite, this standing
outside   in the depth of night

no perfume from Spanish battlements
no ascent of Mount Carmel
no stigmata of lilac wounds
this cloud of unknowing tempered
with signs of your future

this boy in spastic electric hell
of crossfire in the brain
of runes and deadly lesions
(and raven's cry like CaCaCa)
with no lord to wipe the chalk away
this hopscotch drawing firestorms
where they will
down one sphere and up another
crossing the corpus callosum
parody of light
parody of consciousness

parody of converse with the god
and Goddamn it to hell! I scream
rocking you in my arms, blubbering
wailing   keening

and even here you are the patient one
leading by gesture and grace
small arm raised from convulsions
soft hand touching my face
tiny fingers stroking my cheek
and a look   even here in hell
a look   from the midst of your
absence   of love.

Part I
The Helix

3 JULY 1994

Sunday morning but no peignoir
no cockatoos of bold plumage
no scarlet lemon crimson lavender
lime, no herbal oils for crooks
and crannies, for crevices
that never see the sun.

In the cool basement
a remote radio din
sinks through the floorboards;
and in the undersea mimesis
of cobwebs and dust, words
lose their edge and clarity,
consonants swallowed by indifference,
vowels shifting quickly
like schools of fish.
A piano follows the chatter
with easy loping chords of blue,
then a child is heard
repeating over and over again,
"Now what? Now what? Now what?"

If I awoke this morning as Wallace Stevens—
a bag full of poems, lilacs, insurance briefs—
I would still want something else.

Clarity is ephemeral.
A mirror floating on a sea of desire.
Even nothingness hungers
for more nothingness.

"Now what?" I ask, as the boy's small feet
pound towards a ringing phone.
Someone starts a load of wash, the machine
whirrs like a dervish, water sloshing
down the pipes behind me.
This is not Key
West I remind myself,
as if desire could ever transmute a world.

Outside the small window I see tansy,
sedum, daisies—
all blooming yellow and immaculate white—
honeysuckle against the wall
floods the house
with an ethereal fragrance

"Now what?" a woman's voice
in sudden silence—the machines
have all quit, even the radio. But the child's
outside in the sweet summer air,
and today in the sun he will not answer.

19 JUNE 1994: GARDEN OF UNEARTHLY DELIGHTS

walking slowly down D's garden
the sun out at last
forty days and nights it seems of rain
and I'm drifting
slowly out of the storm.
send out a dove, I think
but all I had was pigeons and
they never got past my
frying pan and parsley.

meanwhile D bends over the
weeds rocking slowly on her mexican sandals
her hips and thighs round and fecund
her nose healing slowly
(a deviated septum from a beating at
work) but they took out some bone
and now she looks I swear
like cleopatra
dark exotic beauty
of occult gypsy ways—
I'll be mark anthony to your
queen of the nile, I offer.
no, she counters, smiling
with a fist full of chickweed
you'll be the bear
we chase and kill with dogs.
suddenly I'm on all fours
rolling down the lawn on great padded paws

into the herbs first, snuffling
grinning quietly
three kinds of thyme, tufty purple
chives, smal forests of chamomile—
then the perennials, irises
soapwort, columbine, bleeding hearts
dianthus
my senses raging
through the lavender, maroon, deep blood red
the delicate white of baby's-breath
and bursting suns of *santana matricaria*—
through the wild olfactory
feast of lilac and honeysuckle,
aswarm with aphids.
time to spray, D says
sharply, but I hear
time to spade
and clear out quickly—

indecisive as ever we sit later
on the small back patio worrying
about what to do. move out?
move on? split up?
and what about the boy?

she dreams endlessly of mexico
while I'm partial to cape breton
the queen charlottes, my home on saltspring.
we can't work here that's obvious—
and can't spring the lingo loose
or whip the air with leathery
cant or rise high
with vowels sublime—

no magic here it seems—
just good schools and health care.
just?
the boy comes first
and these trees will have to do

this ring of green from our patio piazza:
a silver birch with leaves like coins
five elms with trunks like dancers stretching
a weeping birch that longs to swim—

these rooted things that never move away.

ALL THE ENERGY IN MUSIC

outside a riot of robins trilling terwillicking in trees
on rooftops and actually running down the long peaks ridges
rooflines—running and singing
for the rain has come again
and again the crazy joy of spring water dripping
off leaf off branch off eaves
off car antenna and chrome bumper—
0 pleroma of worms, they sing
while inside Stan Getz Oscar Peterson in time
to linear splash
of pneumatic tires through puddles
a seamless bass line of rubber
on wet concrete—
then outside to small wartime houses
barely two stories one bath—
though across the street this actress
has two bathrooms two kids two dogs and a husband
who's left and filed for divorce.

her garden will be her salvation—
and may the robin's song soothe
her little boy's seizures—
may
the robin's race endure our own.

IT IS CLEAR

It's clear that Gavin descending the cellar
stairs while I read from Yeats is a meaning
complete in itself. With his fair skin and
twilight eyes, his stocky build and lovely
bare feet on wood, he's more than enough
for this or any lifetime.

What more can I know than this sensible
confluence of beauty? This child I love, this
music bespeaking my heart—*In my golden
house on high*, says Mr.Yeats, *there
they shine eternally.*

DIAPHANEITY, THE VISIBLE ORIGINS

Driven from the house by the mindless joy of
someone else's kids,   I escape to the garden:
the little patch of green I call Paradise.
Hasn't my wife done a nice job? I hear
myself cooing to the pigeons next door:
daisies, portulaca, daffodils and glads.
It's nice enough,   if you don't mind the
wires overhead: Presenting *The Garden,*
by Sask Power and Piet Mondrian.

But the dogs in the alley are barking boors
and the trucks and lawnmowers never stop.
Only in the shed is there quiet enough,
for Pissarro's *Garden With Trees in Blossom,*
Spring, Pontoise—where a stillness
imbues those new white petals   a clear
light breaking free from the ground.

MARTHA'S OLD GALS

Martha's old gals give her more love than
almost anyone.   Mrs. Mitchell, for example,
said one day, while looking out the window,
It's only one sky—yet it rains
here and there.

Mrs. Buchan, on the other hand, said this
about leaving the sprinklers on: *If you*
keep them on long enough   first the canaries
will come   then the bird of paradise.
It's nice she has these frail old blossoms,
for we both despair of the times and the
colour of the planet's aura.   She quotes
as often as she can the following lines:
Whether the shadow becomes our friend or
enemy   depends largely upon ourselves.

In a dry summer, though, it's the sprinkler
that really matters   for shadows run like
ink when the earth turns to rain.   There's
only one sky, we pause to remember   then
come canaries   and the bird of paradise.

THE BREAKFAST OF THE MAGI

Only hours before you gave birth we had breakfast with Liz at that place on the river. Seated near big windows, you were first to see that mallard with the peculiar head. How much like a dinosaur, you said, leaning serenely on the table. Liz concurred, calling all birds *dinosaurish,* while I ordered bacon and extra toast. Our sexual proclivities vary from year to year, but we are totally in agreement on this basic issue: sex is not the most basic issue. Even with one of us bulging at seams, a ripe pink pod, we three are Magi of the Imagination. Slipping through a gate at back of mind—down a green summer trail—going far and golden beyond the walls.

EPIPHANY, SEPTEMBER 1991

Thunderheads boil in from Rosetown
and the multifoliate sky
blossoms forth forms unseen
in a sacristy of silence.
There's not an idea left
that can transverse the span
of the great *IS*, I think.
But heavy rains for May,
even some snow,   and those
greens are richer than ever.

First a time of green—then a
longer time of brown, or yellow-
burnt almond—then finally
white.   Purity like a colour
to put you to sleep.

THE HELIX

1.

Like a shining helix, love brings relief. This is an enviable place to be. In love with Love yet in love with no one. Cowardice? Perhaps, though more of a need for permanent change.

Last night I saw a long pale tunnel winding into my heart. It twisted, so maybe it was simply a reclining cyclone, a secret gyre full of future blessings. But maybe it was like the Ho Chi Minh Trail, bringing needed solace to a poor, oppressed state of affairs.

2.

The last time we made love is the last time we'll make love. There, I've said it!

We may have years left together, but not another second in a wet, heated embrace. This puts us at odds with the age, but I say, "fuck the times." Now is the season for being like a mountain, this final stage for me. No light step through western woods, no molten rutting on a barrel of laughs. Instead, I feel tired bones longing for those gentle corrosives of the earth. Now will be stillness, laughter and quiet.

On my side, with knees drawn up thus, I will lose all knowledge of the gender and shape of my mind.

3.

Today love will rouse me from my bed, grab me by the nose, then lead me to a trough for a cold and heartless dunking. Love does this from time to time; it is part of our contract. I pretend I can't live without her, she pretends I'm not really pretending.

Today love will call with the force of hurricane spring. But I'll be ready, lashed to the mast of my constant ardor, and will pin her with my legs for most of the day. In the evening, and just before the hour of august rebirth, she'll finally wriggle free in a mellower mood. My ripeness awaiting the plunge.

6.

I will be as true to love as love is true to me. No, I'll be truer. I can feel it growing like Italian marble in my heart. There, in the grotto of my unrelinquished faith in love. There, where passing beneath cruel imperium, I feel in the dark for words from the martyrs. This old rough stone must be shaped, they command, marble not worked is marble soon broken.

And I agree, surrendering my love to those voices at night, that their steel might issue a form I can live with.

9.

(for Krista, Brennan, Gavin)

This one small love is all I have left and why complain, it's more than enough. When I wake up early just to watch it rising from sleep; when I hold it close to smell the cleanness of its hair; when I carry it over small rivers and through dark mountain passes; when I do all this, uncomplaining with aches and pains, I know it is more than enough.

Thank you, love, for this hour of your small rebirth.

11.

The problem is, dear love, that the dog is always prowling; wants to sniff, snort, lick, nip, croon canine tunes in beloved's ear, all while mounting a rear assault. That golden cocker with her gypsy shawls and skirts, with her maddening earrings carved from savory bones. The old dog wants new tricks, wants to jump through fiery hoops to save Fifi's favourite rubber toy. That old dog of the senses, driven to baying at this moon of elusive bewildering orgasm. Wolfen on the trail—keen scented snout.

The problem is, love, old rover loves to hunt.

12.

It went like this: a weird light filled the cab of my jeep, a rosy luminescence pouring from a globe in the centre of my chest. Then the top of the silver sphere retracted, to reveal ancient spires and crenelated walls. Yes, this is the realm of the loving soul, the ruby light affirmed: paradise, bliss, the *aurora hora*. This is *real,* it sagely murmured.

So I drove on slowly, both eyes glued to the icy road. And the rosy dawn held against black silhouettes, slumbering trees and the bleak winter cold.

15.

In Cecil Green's old mansion at university, I tried gallantly to learn Chopin's "Tristesse." You sat patient in the shadows, never once recoiled when my clumsy fingers broke the spell of beauty. Quietly you sat with the view: English Bay, Georgia Strait, the islands north towards Howe Sound. Some said your hair was thin and mousy, your complexion dry, your demeanor that of a Magyar peasant. But in your eyes, love, there was a world like an endless sea. And in your suffering was a promise of paradise just over the horizon. When you withdrew that promise, I fought back with everything I had: a very bad reading of Chopin's sonorous virtue.

Please forgive the dissonance of those last few hours. "Tristesse" is indestructible, and so are you.

16.

I'm standing in a small prairie market, looking through a big picture window at the blue winter sky. Turning around, I see a man beside me staring out into the azure. A youngish man with Sam Beckett eyes and face. Suddenly, among the bananas, I realize that all around the world, at this very moment, millions of hearts are pouring out their windows. Waiting and wondering. And there we are as well, the Beckett-looking man and I: gazing up into the warm thawing blue. The chinook-washed sky of gentle mid-winter blessing. When they ring up my apples, tomatoes, broccoli and fish, dear love, I thank heaven for these small and worldly favours.

18.

Love, there is a place where you are mentioned only in the first person, as if no distance ever came between you and a beating heart. This is the realm of the angels, the mad and glorious seraphim. In this place of love-in-the-first-person, there was a minor cherub who had a terrible dream about life without you. Yes, relegated to the second person, love became a shadow of its former glory: a fleeting glimmer passing between the eyes of the dead and dying. The cherub was so frightened he passed out of existence, leaving only his dream as a warning.

Have you ever heard of such a place? Do you really know how we might wake up? Would you please scratch my back where the wings used to be?

O VIRGINIA

The Virginia Woolf scholar from North Carolina
is a slight gentle woman with intelligent eyes;
beautiful too, though her mind is what first
impresses. That and the economy
of her simple dress:
Mao trousers sneakers embroidered
cotton shirt.
She's uncomfortable with the clumsiness
of northern men,
how they don't make room
when you walk
down the walk, forcing you off
into mud and snow.

"Manners are of utmost importance,"
she quotes from Malory.
But her world is also deeper
as when astonished by
a flight of swans
she's digging spuds in her garden
by the river.

THE POET AND FRIENDS

Your poems are never simple enough, she
said, easing his arm from her shoulder—
why can't you write like this guy?   Here
this one's beautiful: someone slept
with his wife, his best friend in fact,
and someone else cut off their foot.
See?   The stitches are so real
they make you shiver with the needle.
Your stuff makes me dizzy—and
when you read them, all you want is
approval.   If I say what I think
you just hit the roof.

OK, he said, you're right—I'm
a bad-tempered prick with a fiery tongue.
With your crinoline wings all scorched
and black, how will you ever fly?
Never, she said, I never will—
but the weight of your head on the
base of my spine keeps me straight
on the road that I'm running.

THE ROUND OF LOVE

He loved her and I loved her and someone else once loved her and who does she love? Woman, thy name is whispered in the court of the rose; thy name is Temptress, also Mother, Sister, Nun and Whore. He once loved her but she threw him over, then I loved her for awhile but she tired of my wheezing. Waltzes are beautiful things, she said, but you can turn them into endurance contests. She now loves someone else, though still loving me in a special way—I love you, she says, but I'm not IN love with you. I thank her for those meager crumbs, I thank her for letting me phone on Sunday afternoons—she is awake by then, usually, has showered, and is lying on cushions with a view of both sea and mountains. Avoid caviar, she advises, you know how it gives you gas. I take her counsel, seriously too, for I'm IN love with another who'll maybe love me—we'll see.

THE ETIQUETTE OF EATING FROM THE OCEAN

When prying open the soft-shelled mollusk
warm gently by rubbing and applying
light pressure. Also, kelp and rockweed
may be hiding the lips, the portal
to the soft tasty centre within.

Gently disentangle such salty wet
strands, and never thrust intrusively.
Rather, tickle lightly the mollusk's
delicate antenna, then watch it
gasp open in delight. Apply butter
and consume. Lobster bib optional.

Part II

Aniko *and* Other Poets

EXTINCTION ODE: FOR PANSIES

From this time of tongues we pull hymns, rhymes and nursery
songs   for dinosaurs are in the dahlias and serpents are in the
sunflowers.   These are the last times, the violets seem to say,
these are the final hours for cornflowers and forget-me-nots.
And whose children are these? you thornily ask.   They're
yours and mine, for all children belong   even oxeye daisies.

All forms of light are mine! saith the Flower God, like fleabane
and the vaginal rose called carnation. But the big scaly feet
of the terrible lizards trample all the dream gardens and make
the kids scream! No wonder they suffer from terminal night-
mares, no wonder they sleep at their desks during class. What's
this bullshit, you say, they're only flowers! But please, never say
only flowers, for the water lily once was your mother's placenta—
the Nymphaea fruit you feed on at night.

ANIKO/ONE

I don't think I've ever told you why I like Greek food wrapped in vine leaves, she said, and we said, no, you haven't. Well, it was long ago when I was just a girl, she continued, in her polished apple way, and we parked mugs of tea on the picnic table, lit pipes and smiled, our minds roaming back to before the Second World War. I was not quite sixteen, and went down to London to visit my sister and her boyfriend, Kurt, the German-Jew—I felt very pleased with myself, for all the reasons girls do when they're almost sixteen and travelling alone in the big safe world. They were marvellous hosts, and took me to Soho to a Greek place where Kurt fell almost immediately in love with me. And my sister, who had many boyfriends, and was engaged fifteen times before she finally married, went upstairs to find a bathroom. Finding a long queue of young women, she went to the end of the line to await her turn. But it wasn't a line for the bathroom after all—it was a recruitment station for whores bound for South America.

Well, my sister laughed so hard she couldn't pee, and came downstairs in rollicking agony. Soon we were all laughing and made our way out of the café where, much to our surprise, the Maltese chef was stabbed to death right before our eyes. Another Maltese came running up behind him and stabbed him in the back—swoosh, right through the heart. It was the first murder I ever witnessed and I was understandably shaken—but it was also the beginning of a most marvellous affair, and even better because Kurt sent me books. I remember getting *Howard's End*, by Forster, and being very pleased as it was one of the first Penguin paperbacks. Kurt eventually went back to Germany, and I think he must have died there during the war. So, whenever I eat anything rolled up in vine leaves, I think fondly of him—savouring the foliage of our dulcet love.

ANIKO/TWO

Most writers out here write into
the landscape, she said, peering
into her goldfish pond. I write
out of it—which makes sense
when you think about it. She's
the only grandmother in town
reading *Cosmology and the New
Physics*. I'm really a Blakean,
you know, she muttered one day,
ladling out ratatouille—*the
body is the emanation of the spirit.*
Eternity always now.

ANIKO/FOUR

When driving the hot summer prairie, she said, you used to come to these old cafés—all pretty much the same, painted bilious green, with high ceilings and big rotating fans. You'd pile in and order pie and coke, and the heat inside was every bit as bad as the hell you'd just driven through. There was even a joke about drivers on the prairies—how their arms came off with the doors. But it was the only way to keep cool out there: hanging out a window catching every little breeze.

There's nothing like driving on those far southern flats, she continued. While the heat seems to put your body to sleep, your mind climbs up a shimmering blue sky—*the most spiritual landscape in the world.*

5 AUGUST 1994

Yesterday
walked through the vast park
that is part of this retreat centre—
many trails led
down from the Franciscan House
into a valley that climbed,
on the other side
to a highway running south to Regina.

Spreading dense bush of small birch
poplar alder willow by the creek
the occasional spruce or pine—
and berry thickets everywhere
food for birds small hidden spaces
where deer hide until dusk
and flowers proliferate in the tall
golden grasses:
brown-eyed susans
blue prairie asters and
delicate alfalfa flower
then finally with wild purple coif
bergamot.

Another writer comes down the trail
as I climb up
swinging my canvas hat
at various bugs—
I can't see any insects,
she says
strolling confidently past.

Later I see her running
for cover
pursued by swarms of flies and mosquitoes
her red shorts disguising
the blood
of the bugs she has crushed.

What would Francis do with Mosquitoes?
Come Sister Mosquito, come
Brother Musca Fly
come feast on my savory juices?

Where will I go when everything
comes tumbling down around me?
I no longer have the energy
to keep anything erect. And
every pose within me
wants to lie down and sleep
for half eternity.

The parent wants to sleep
the husband wants to sleep
the lover's been asleep for a decade
the intellectual wants
nothing more than to put out his lamp
the writer's gone blind
the saint has lost sight of
Jerusalem.

I will embrace the Buddha of Repose;
I will wear
pajamas woven from clouds.
Silence will seal my house.

THE PRACTICE OF DEPTH

She said *dabbling in Aristotle would make a cute title for a book,* and I thought hhhmnnn, just like a woman—or just like this woman, to be exact. Baby, when will you learn how to flow? What we thought was arthritis is just the long-term effect of your much-too-editorial mind. Now the Presocratics, that's another matter—*dabbling in the Presocratics,* what a fine and impossible thing. Why you can't just dabble in all that ontological gas—it's quicksand! It's the primordial stuff! One spark and you're up in flames.

I've been burnt a few times, so I know what I'm talking about. Walking around Smithers and Houston with a mind full of roaring butterflies, my projects devoured by a calico sky—It's the new consciousness, girl, and there's nothing new under the moon. Now take Heraclitus, for in/stance: how're you going to make it with a cat who buries himself in a dung pile? In all your years throwing back mint juleps, you never once were asked to dig shit. How offal, you would have cried, holding a nose-gay of poems to your delicate muzzle.

OBIT(E)UARY

the boy with the big bones eventually came unglued
and they laid him in the quiet green blankets of spring
like a brisket too long in the oven . . . a remarkable
smell really   onions carrots parsley peppers his ex-
panding skin seemed cool to the touch bones gently
sliding and slipping through muscle and sinew   they
gathered like the clans at knees and ankles   though
the skull remained intact for a time   and his visage
filled with a tapering light from the body's blight . . .
good food, he said, good friends   what more can i
ask for?   proceeding then to pass out the silver
a lovely table set for eight   and he closed tight
his eyes as they tucked in their napkins   and put
slices of orange over the glass of his soul.

BLACK

be still and know God, and you do   and He is . . .
but then one day it happens   on your chest sits
silence   and though your faith is like unto
a mustard seed   nothing you do shall lift that weight.

be still, know nothing   and you do, and it is
no longer like a place to voyage from   no longer
like a walk to damascus . . . a weight sits
on your chest   and you die without speaking:
the death much darker
                                        than black magnolia.

NO TRAPDOOR IN THE CROSS

and you watched him climbing the steeple of st john the divine
with his hammer nails sheets of plywood pots of glue and paint
these are the simple servants of your will   he called to the
clouds and hazy dawn   i am your simple servant and have dominion
over all the rest

then you watched him climb to the steeple top like a bowery
weather vane   old ragged suit jacket dungarees tartan slippers
broken down in the heels   and there he perched glowing in the
aureate rays around him   balancing two-by-fours on the cross
driving spikes into plywood palms   whirling paint like a
new creation

it rose   and you saw it rising high in the sky   clouds parting
in reverence for his new age triptych   trisecting the heavens
in case the one actually was three   not wanting to leave anyone
out   and look! a special recliner for mary   rocking in the
stiff winds she'll rock to her sacred heart's content   with
her babe

i watched crowds gathering below   dumbfounded before the mira-
culous   this erection thirty stories high above hot dogs spandex
girls and boys on rollerskates and chariot boards   javelins in
their flamingo hair   the deadly darts held sharp and lethal
with axle grease

how can he keep the whole thing up there?   someone marvelled
that big hinged window must weigh a ton   then we all fell on
our faces in terror   but thrilled like tykes on christmas morn
something was peeking through the window   gazing down from
himalayan heights   blinking rubbing sleep from his eyes . . .

the god has awakened! the crowd sang out   hymnals dug out of
old cabbage crates   people falling to their knees for practice
as hookers pulled up their skirts to curtsy and cops and punks
forgave each other with the kiss of peace

so then you called out, how come god looks like a bowery bum?
and sure enough   you could see the tattered suit coat   the
grubby stubbled chin   and when god stood on his head for phle-
bitus   well there were his floppy tartan slippers   out in the
toe and grimier than hell . . . it was a mirror!   the old man
had raised a mirror

everybody was sour at your revelation   and who could blame them?
as by the thousands they woefully retired   hymnals back in the
cabbage crates hookers back on the streets   what a dirty trick!
only out of some perverse curiosity   you and i remained   watched
the bum smile one last time   watched the mirror light up   then
he climbed through the frame before it all disappeared . . .
there's a trapdoor in the cross   you muttered to yourself
but you didn't half-believe it   and neither do i

THE 'I GO' STORY

I go to the station to meet anyone who needs to be met
for I know what it's like to arrive at an empty station.
It doesn't matter how far you've travelled sometimes it's
just a trip to the store for cigars and a loaf of bread
or a quiet walk under rugged elm trees   feet dragging in
the snow   chickadees shining in the moonlit freeze.   Re-
turning after a walk like that you wish more than anything
that someone nice might be inside   making hot chocolate
arranging your slippers   laying out your dressing gown.
Yes   you arrive back home after strolling in the winter
world and you want nothing more than the smell of freshly
baked bread   cooling on the counter   and as you put on
slippers and dressing gown someone comes to greet you
with a nice new cigar.

Why do I go on like this?   The tomb is empty, he rose
from the dead   he rose from the dead and climbed into
heaven and I wasn't there to say goodbye.   Can you im-
agine what it's like   going on a trip with no one there
to see you off?   I would have waved longer than anyone
none of your usual bored and perfunctory flaps   I know
what it's like to be sent off like that.   And you get
home after touring the frozen world   and the tomb's still
barren   and there are no angels baking bread, arranging
slippers   or hiding cigars in dressing gown pockets.

A wise man said that Grace is Meeting . . . and so I go
briskly to anything which needs to be met   stepping
up to the station . . .

BOTTLE, BOX, CIRCLE SQUARED

(for Helen Jean)

the old woman lived adequately but in a box that no one
could see her days fashioned from the woes of times past
and her voice never so alive as when counting and binding
old pains and troubles. an old man figured in most of
them and while she lived in a box he lived in a bottle
pickled much of the time it's true but also like a small
model ship yearning for blue wide open seas . . .

there had been some form to his life he had seen men die
and often tried to think when the pain would allow but
the two of them still lived on as friends one in a box
one in a bottle and though often far apart in different
worlds the telephone was there and on holidays and high
feast days he would leave his glass tower and liquid green
hills and set forth to visit her dark box of sorrows . . .

where windows would open like eyes for the dawn bright
curtains appear, nasturtiums in pots then a hand of cards
at the old kitchen table (rummy, her favourite game) with
mumbled spells passed round for love and an awkward hug
at the end of each hand . . . i wish it was different! they'd
both exclaim, but didn't we have a ton o'laughs and how're
the kids, their pets and grandkids? and how's the old gang?
old friends are the best! then slowly he'd sink into
mickey and mix slowly she'd drift into fruitless quiet . . .
and that would be that for another year. square peg
round hole bottle and box.

PENMANSHIP AND SALVATION

Mrs. Hunt! Thank you for those hard hours sweating
over McLean's Method of Penmanship. No one could
make mandalas like you on the board, cosmic pies
hurtling across the dark green sky.   On Fridays
we'd use coloured chalk, like carnival time, but
you kept us on our sacred path: circles, ovals,
loops, spirals—all that we might do ourselves
proud in the reticular eyes of Mr. McLean . . .

Today Mrs. Hunt, years after you drove your
white Falcon coupe straight to heaven—today,
with Mater Matter writhing under Man's malevolent
touch—today Mistress Hunt, dear Athena of the
Ink Wells, I make circles in your honour.
Perfect rings to heal my hands:
Imago Terra Nova.

ONLY FOR BRIDESMAIDS

in the dark the first time there were awkward instructions
place your hand here, yes, that's it   place your lips here
then kiss   or lick—one of them was new and one old
in the loving arts

yes, she said, that felt good   and to think i'd never ever
dreamed of this   that it ever really happened   that one
woman could lay with, another   so salty, so sweet

the other reclined thinking of a smoke   tomorrow's sermon
drifting through her mind like incense   she was a bride of
the lord and a bride of the flesh   and saved herself only
for bridesmaids

i am thinking of martha and mary, she said   and how they
are really one woman caught in a bind   the lord saith, yes
mary, sit here please   but for martha there was bread to
bake   laundry to do   apostles to humour

i am the very reverend martha/mary   i am whore repentant
virgin perpetual   assumed to be now in heaven   i am all of
these with a brain to boot   but do you think they take me
seriously?   the men only wonder who'll take communion
when i'm on the rag!   you'd think they all were lunatics,
so obsessed with my monthlies!

DIRT AND THE HOLY

A cold winter night but clear, with strong winds drying
the last of the crops. Wheat off tonight, tomorrow the
rape. And how fine being dirty on a last harvest eve,
the strong smell of diesel spilling over my hands,
dragging me back to a primal world. Mystery is where
it's coming from, mystery is where it's going . . . and
the coyotes feel it crying late in their dens, and the geese
in the sky the trout in the slough, all leaping and
flapping from deep in their rites, enacting the soundless
brilliant laughter. Or like me just filling an old diesel
drum, careless with wonder in the midst of it all.

VOX STUPENDUS

The Voice is the body of Christ, says the dream
then asks, *But who is Christ?*

Rising through the elements, the given forms
of mater materia, rising through the columns
of cups, pentacles, wands and swords—

the Voice of the body, given
as blood and wine
a sacrament of speech

lifting light to the lips, and lips
to the heart's four quarters
that domain of perfect silence.

<O>

Here in the court of the faceless god
at the feet of whom "a storm of white"
rising, lifting, winning . . .

The voice is the body of the soul, says the dream
then asks, *But what is not the body?*

"Rising through orders not yet blessed
the Voice sings choirs of carnal bliss,
like lovers rising to kiss the seed
at the foot of the holy rood."

<O>

Then flight, where the heart is mirrored
at the back of the eye, where an image
of light dissolves the world . . .

Who am I to dream of a singing speech,
stuttering before the altar, a stammered
syntax with wringing hands?

But even I can be forgiven. Mouth of all
unholy pursuits. Even I can stand clear
for a quick line breaking
at the center of speech.

<O>

(Foxes in the cedar shrubs. Geese in the lilies.
Man in the woman he's taken to love.)

This is what I am, says the voice—
a delivery at the core of love.

Dear Bb,

My mind is growing a huge translucent bulb on its trunk;
I think something like a tulip in the making, an enormous
yellow tulip. This huge luminous bloom will be seen only
by those with invisible eyes. *There goes Ron,* you will say,
*with his handsome yellow tulip. See how it bounces bravely in the
wind. See how angels tease it with hot coals, and how the flower
turns towards All Eternity*. I am happier than ever and nearly
dead. Like Ponce de Leon with a water-witch, I gladly expire
in Paradise. All I need know is this aching void and the glory
of sunlit flowers:

compost in the roots of a starry blossom.

Dear Dd,

The Buddha's wife came to me last night in dream, with a message I think you'll want to hear. First, let me describe her most recent incarnation: about five feet eight inches, forty-ish, fair-skinned, with a limp from phlebitis, an overbite and fairly weak chin. She had a lovely voice, though, and seemed happy in spite of bruises on her face and arms. *Pain is forever,* she intoned poetically, striking a pose with eight arms akimbo. *Pain is for keeps and bliss is forever, where the two of them meet you shall finally be free.* Then she kissed my cheek and slowly turned away to a darkened closet. Wait! I cried, not wanting to be alone and awake in the shadows. Wait, please, Miss—*Mrs.*, she said, *Mrs. Buddha, but call me Eileen.* That's pretty, I trembled, sounds Irish. But she slipped through the void with no word of return.

from *FLOWERING CHEWNOWSKY, BIRTHWORT AND ALL*

4.

Chewnowsky high on Sumas Mountain, flopped in the
midst of pines and alders, talking to his gods, as Gauguin
stars blow angel dust on the breast of his navy peacoat.
Sweet August airs in the handsome hermit bush: grasses,
seeds, needles, cones, all crushed beneath his rugby frame.
Chewnowsky's tears for the Holy one's. Hoplite and line-
backer, number seventy-four, crying aloud for the Beautiful
things: for three sad chords from Suzanne's song about love,
green tea, and lush bruised oranges.

5.

Old Chewer on the playing field, not Eton but Panther heaven, with football helmets crashing, smelly, sweaty pads and boots, cleats tearing turf and skin—DIG! DIG! DIG! screams the coach, and everyone digs in, legs braced, helmets minus plumes like Thermopylae. Chew on the bench, then combing his locks and into the breach for a charge! WHAM! BAM! WHAM! Victory loss, a few dead Spartans, nothing matters, only Beauty. The sun-golden curvaceous forms of the Chorus: tanned laconic lovelies turning cartwheels in the twilight, each one capable of launching a thousand punts.

Chewnowsky dreams of emulating Paris, of stealing the best of them all—platinum Magyar bombshell, a letter sweater girl, and how those primary vowels bend space and time across her bosom: the AAA, the OOO, the festoon of delighting dugs. Chew bleeds everywhere he can, now collapsing with cleat stigmata on breast, awaiting Red Cross pallet with sighs. But the chorus moves on, leaving nothing but silence in the fertile land—broad river to the north, Mount Baker to the south—while huge cottonwoods, in a bog behind the school, roll fleecy white seed pods to mend his wounds. Chewnowsky left solo on a field of desire, quill pen poised for any sign of the Muse.

7.

DREAM 1: Chewnowsky in basketball heaven: a pure shiny floor of perfect waxed oak; zones of shifting coloured lines, not straight but Celtic knots; worm Ouroboros in blue and green, gulping down tail under ruby red eyes; a god racked with antlers at the top of the key.

Dribbling a full moon the length of the gym, Chewnowsky goes up for a basket, but the hoop disappears in a volley of sunspots, then the key melts down and the court as well. When the Mysterium vanishes altogether, Chewie wakes up gasping and lost, with those blue-eyed belles now sweat soaked pillows and itchy green blankets. His choice of tuning in to radiant Being is abruptly caught short of pneuma, the breath.

12.

NIGHTMARE 1:

Chewnowsky in pedagogical hell, like Dungeons and Dragons with no magic for the players. Here is where the young soul first appears: in body, in school. Here is where the young soul first surrenders its bliss: always colouring within lines, while the Sacred Heart of Jesus jumps rope in the schoolyard, daring anyone to use His name in vain. Who are these denizens not extramundane but extraordinarily mundane? Who are these chalk marks passing for people? Vertical in all the right ways (posture, deportment, penmanship), but closed off at the pineal gland: at Magritte's opening glory; at Rimbaud's magical beans. And this plant that grows so much like Posey—deep-rooted, titan-trunked—this green sinewy gift of God takes Chewnowsky from out of the schools, leaving notes from parents and concerned seraphim: *Dear School,* the notes read antiphonally, *please excuse Master Chew from class today as it is imperative he awaken to his true birthright: by lily and birthwort, by Trillium erectum, becoming both Bard and Anthropos as quickly as possible.*

Yours truly, the Real Deal

But sirens go off, and bells; janitors awaken with brooms in ruddy fists; principals with leather straps and counsellors—bleary-eyed, lost—with tomes on the ocular evils of masturbation. Peg-legged Scottish historians, Mennonite giants with happy versions of *The Waste Land,* gentleman farmers in harness, bald pates, eagle-beaked with mole-vision; both male and female they awaken to the alarm; track coach castrati with shot balls chained to their minds. *Grab your axes!* the principal cries, *greening is amongst us, the sinister pangs of rebirth.*

And Chewnowsky slowly comes to light miles above the Valley: to the din of distant commands and ringing axes; to a living death attacking the Tree; to the very real terror of distance and the fall. Chewnowsky then falls with the dying plant, but the Muse keeps his eyes at the top of the sky—for Trillium erectum, birthwort and all.

Part III

The Art Catalogue

THE ART CATALOUGE

1.

In Henri Rousseau's *The Sleeping Gypsy*, we are treated to the evocative magic of a colourfully robed girl being nuzzled by a lion as she sleeps. The magic, of course, stems not so much from these innocent figures as from the use of shading and light, a technique peculiar to "La Douanier." His created stillness and rounded fullness seem to draw forth each *thing* from the depths of the ontological mystery itself. I bring this painting to your attention, dearest, because it seems to brilliantly capture the mood of our relationship. Please, please, no accusations of morbidity—it may not be the end. And as the moon shines over my shaggy head and neck, as I rise from our bed in the misshapen form of a poorly drafted lion, please be aware of my calling: prophet, seer, shaman, poet! May the moon ever be my guide. I give you one last kiss, praying deeply that my carnivore's breath will not disturb you.

But all of this is beside the fact—I've changed, and in a major way. It's the end of our ordinary life together; yet from the haunting stillness of this landscape may come another kind of love. And the light falling from that bright full moon, softly curling down the thick blue air—I may yet walk higher upon it, and you, when you awaken, may follow.

2.

I stand corrected—surprisingly enough, it's a woman in Pierre Bonnard's *Dining Room on the Garden*: it's his beloved wife, Marthe, anchoring the composition with her "elegant dark clothes." How was I to know? The cheap bastard's only got her painted three-quarter length, probably to save on material. And her hair, a few gay strokes pulled back lost in the bright orange wall. For a minute there, I thought it was a boy about twelve years old, certainly no more than thirteen. It's a bold, beautiful day outside, with the sea and sky intensifying one another in the window: blue turning to green, violet to turquoise. The clear sharp colours of the trees leap at one's eyes like predatory limes; they fill the soul with chlorophyll, and the God-breath within goes aaahhhh! But the fat little boy thinks only of his broken heart. On the table there are jam-pots, fruit, a jug of cool milk and cheerful yellow swirls that could be tasty lemon sticky buns. The pudgy swain quickly forgets his aching aorta, surrendering to the riches of the sumptuous sideboard.

His father is away at sea, in disgrace because of several swollen maids. His mother is at Mass, pouring forth her rank and fermented soul to some confessional's grill. Who is for the boy? He'd hoped that love would find his uncommonly deep footsteps in the wet sand. He had plans, romantic and hermetic concoctions full of flimsy silk and lace. He'd sleep with his sabre ready. Beware the Barbary Coast! Beware all pirates and gym instructors! A slender, dark-haired beauty would sink to his knees by the sea-spray; the sensual rhythm of the waves would lull them both to sleep, where they'd dream only of a world full of love and pistachio fudge. All eroticism sublimated, he would never dream of peeking beneath her floral shift, damp from the foaming tides, warm from preening Sol. But in several months of trudging up and down the beach, such a vision never once appeared.

It was now the end of his summer vacation. How would he endure another year in the city? Concrete and sneers, jibes from bus windows whizzing past. The viscous, buttery dreams called to him in their private tongue: a happy belly is worth more than two empty hearts, they sang. And while the ghost of love stands phallic and shiny behind Mrs. Bonnard's favourite chair, the boy-woman descends on the crumpets with a vengeance. This painter knew more than most about eating disorders, as demonstrated by the vertical and horizontal lines accentuating the order and stability of the feast. Yes, he says, drool on fat prince, then sate your desire—Love calls to you from a scintillating interior, the ocular heart.

3.

Now for something about orchids. In Titian's *The Venus of Urbino,* we are treated to the tender sight of a beautiful young woman lightly stroking her pelt. Perhaps she is unaware of our gaze, and who amongst us will break through the crystal reverie of her stainless passion? We are also reminded that this painting was commissioned by the Duke of Urbino—hence, its name—and that it's very reminiscent of a pagan altar piece. Clearly, it worships female sexuality and presents the Goddess of Love as an earthly woman, aware of her beauty and the physical pleasures of life's fragrant garden.

Yes, aaahh, the pleasures—*Life through coloured light* is a phrase often employed to describe Titian's luminous surfaces, and the warm glow of this beauty's skin is enhanced by creamy gold tints in the sheet and pillows of her couch. Notice, also, dangling from her left ear and catching the light off her cheek, a small crystal that will appear centuries later in a Vancouver psychic shop. But who has time for gossip? Suffice it to say, it will be worn by members of either sex at various poetry readings. Perhaps that is why the maidservants are in a panic in the background, one of them diving headfirst into the bottom of a large trunk. The future is frightening for the working class. They must be assured at all times of the stable condition of reality. And what could be more reassuring than a small, confining space? But we digress—who cares where and how that earring finally disappeared, falling down a toilet at a gallery? Titian would have approved, what with his *radiant confidence and enjoyment of life.*

4.

Most mystifying is the way the young starlet's hand covers her groin, supposedly a traditional pose: I'm almost certain she's fingering her clit. Oh, don't get me wrong — I don't disapprove in the least; it's just that it's so damned difficult to describe, in a literary sense. Now I know of several healthy women poets who have written paeans in praise of penises, and these poems are very fine and treat the member-in-hand in a playful, yet most respectful way. But what can the male bard do in return, what do we call female genitalia? Especially in an age retreating resolutely from the folly of machismo. Cunt? So violent, so brutal—the Venus of Urbino can be seen playfully fluttering her languorous "cunt?" And then you quickly add that the emerald curtain background acts as a cool dark foil to her skin, its soft folds accentuating the voluptuous lines of her body. Even a little dog at the end of her couch looks mildly bemused at our dilemma. Vagina, beaver, fragrant garden, bearded clam? None of these suffice, damn it, and the eyes of this golden beauty mock us as we twist our minds to accommodate her charisma. Those dark almond-shaped eyes, both provocative and knowing, so radiant in the power of her sexual attraction—alas and alack! Poor tool, our language, poor tool!

Dear Vincent van Gogh,

I am truly entranced by *Starry Night, Saint-Remy* and am writing to inquire about lodgings in your village. It would be discourteous and false of me to pretend that I'm new to this scene. I am no stranger, let me assure you, for on many occasions I have stolen into your tableau for a few days rest. The hut nearest the cypresses, the one with sagging roof and darkened windows, that is where I have lain. A thin mattress, a blanket, a good dark rye and some cheese: these have been my humble friends. One evening I actually stood with the parish priest, helping him count stars in your swirling firmament. He told me about your early years as lay preacher and missionary in Belgium, how the savage tribes of that region tied you to a stake and forced you to recant your beliefs. With the aid of a hot coal fire, they drove you over the edge—but what a wonderful way to fall and what forces it released. This world come to life like a huge coiling cosmic dragon, while the works of man huddle humble and small. In closing, I'd like a very long lease on that dwelling by the trees; then I'll track your rash spirit from the hills to the sky.

Dear Georges Braque,

I have come to suspect that in your masterpiece, *Violin and Palette*, there's to be found an exit from this world of illusion and damnation. Near the bottom right-hand corner, a dark hand points upward to a barely discernible trail leading out through these cold, imprisoning planes. But first I pause to pay tribute to the violin itself, from whose tortured hip springs the instrument of my salvation. As I witness this modern miracle, this flat painted surface on which to reckon the marvel of three-dimensionality, I'm reminded that for every victory there is a price. And of course, I refer to that martyred palette whose sad, unyielding face hangs from the most terrifying nail in creation. The conventional realism of the nail and its shadow serves only to remind us of the ubiquity of evil, and the disturbing closeness of its commonality. But in spite of this or, perhaps, because of this, there rises before me a singular way to higher being: symbolized by the mountain or long green curtain that folds upward behind the victim's mournful visage. Holy mountain or drapes, Mister Braque, does it really make a difference? Or if it does, could you try to be more specific in the future?

Dear Edvard Munch,

I am struck by the figure in your famous painting *The Scream*, completed late in the nineteenth century. In this work, there appears a genderless person who—with some curly black hair, naturally rosy cheeks and piercing blue eyes—would double for a lover of mine: Vancouver, circa 1975. Her life was troubled in many ways, having married a mean mathematician who often threatened her with a knife. But our covert love was sweet, if brief, and when she later became pregnant with her husband's child, she blossomed like no one expected. The baby was a godly gift, a precious pearl in the arid field of their marriage, and together they reached out for a world without shadows. Crib death brought them up short, however, and we all stood by like ghostly mourners. Animal yelps and howling broke the composure of the night, and her shrieks tore through the trees like the keening of a soul without language. Did she tear her hair out by its roots, Munch, and did the colour of her skin seek assurance in the tones of the dead? In time, only the sky was left bleeding, and then the darkness of the earth wrenched her heart out through her mouth.

THE KID'S ON FIRE

And the night progresses with a great blues band
swinging on the stand: hoodoo horns, wild rhythms
but best of all a youngster from black Chicago town
totally wicked on lead guitar. Hermes! we cry from
our tables, being literary men, Hermes! what's new
with the gods? He just smiles and I think, boy,
if this kid don't get laid tonight, there's some-
thing fundamentally wrong with this town. But he
just keeps playing every lick that's ever been
imagined, keeping Whitehead's God in mind, and that
old *infinite possibility* zaps us through lightning
bolt strings, and we're all yelling Fire, Fire, the
kid's on Fire! The joint's on Fire! And what with
all the eye-balling going on, I don't think we're
lying. But the owner thinks we're trying to cause
a riot, which is true, being anarchists and all, so
they boot us out! But that's OK with the bards,
cuz by now we all know the words—*little red
rooster doin' fine.*

NOVENA FOR GRACE KELLY

So there's poor Raymond Burr standing in the darkened doorway
and Jimmy Stewart sitting cold and quiet, though really scared
shitless—What do you want? Thorwald says, Money? I have
none. But Jimmy's got Grace Kelly and what more could you want?
No one ever looked as beautiful as her in *Rear Window*, and even
now with her comely bones resting in state, with thin grim men
weeping calmly over her grave, we still remember. This novena
is especially for her—for the most stunning profile this side of Eve.

How many times have I seen that picture? That perfect
jawline running exquisitely up to her ear, the consummate tilt
of her pert nose? Poor Thorwald had no money, and Raymond
Burr, the dignified Canuck, never got a chance to make love to
Gracy. Somehow he stands for all overweight lunkheads, tied to
nagging harpies around the world. He's the existential hero of
Western cinema. The loud broad always making fun of his suit,
throwing dinner in his boring face, the chops he'd spent hours
on, complete with plastic tulip. As if she could do better: on
her butt all day while Thorwald's out hustling cheap baubles.
No one ever told him life was like this—he should never have
left the farm in Matsqui. Just a few scrubby acres, but at
least he'd have some self-respect. Even now, with Grace
just dust in a jar.

SO FRIGGIN' BLUE

It's funny for a while, then not so funny, then downright
fucking blue. You say the phases of a biochemical
moon run through our blood! Maybe, but last night in
the tub I had to put down the book I was reading—
peeping from the back of my head was a diamond light
bigger'n your fist. *O Bliss!* I sang, breathin' deep
through my nose, then chanting *OM MANI PADME HUM!*
OH MOMMA, MOMMA PLEASE COME HOME!

Having a cold, my septum made a noise like an oboe,
so I played myself for a while, then took to begging.
this sweet light to stay (which it didn't) and the
bath cooled off and I thought of my friends in
Vancouver. My lover on the streets—how she
won't come home. Then I wept and wept
so friggin' blue.

BOTTLED BLUES

sometimes overcome by the grimness of life
the old man would leave his glassy green hills
sing a few songs and travel the roads . . .
some of them he'd even built himself and they
were endless to the eye   with log bridges strung
over raging blue rivers   deep in the bush.

but the music he sang always took him downtown
real sharp in western shirt and boots   where a
waitress would pass him a bubble of kindness
and a spell would decant from the wound
in his heart   like honey all over her lap:
"hey sugar babe   what's new little sweetie?"
not shelley or keats   but it sure did the trick
in smithers, prince george and houston.

if they didn't laugh right away and throw him out
they were lost   and woke up dreaming of log
drawbridges and castles with emerald walls
an old man beside them   snorting and farting.
"my heart," he'd say   "a small trick in the valves."
and the girls would smile   "you did fine old dad."
not telling him how he'd just gone to sleep
the broken little soldier put back in his tent
all quiet that night on the western front.

FOUR STUDIES: CONFIGURING LOVE

(pour ma belle muse de la gare)

1.

Until I was twenty-nine years old, I thought silence was
the language of Love.
At thirty, I thought it was Hungarian
and ardently pursued the tongue of the Magyar (for the
better part of three months, at least).
At forty-one, the
language of Love seems something evolving in the future
of the species. All humans being heirs to a marvel
not yet born.

The sound of Love will be a parlance like no other in existence. Bypassing both lips and
mind, it will enter the heart like the singing of Seraphim.

Like Esperanto, it will be understood all around the world;

unlike Esperanto, it will not sound like lobsters fucking
in the bottom of an old metal dory.

2.

In the movies, we watched gangsters make love to beautiful
women, pull casinos out of the barren hermit desert, and
finally
paint abstract expressionist art on the walls of
empty houses. Their bloodied brains exploded onto the pure
white surfaces
like ideas from the genius of Jackson Pollock,
while bullet holes in the canvas reminded us that life is
short and love almost impossible to achieve.

Did I tell you,
then, that I loved you? Perhaps not, for who can tell the
time when the bells are always chiming. But I do love you
still,
and promise not to frighten you with poems about
my undying ardor.
It'll go when I go, I promise.

3.

How much like Vancouver was our city when the ice-crystals
came like fog among the buildings, cars and cedars. We might
have been walking down Granville on our way to the bar. In
your black leather mini and butterfly stockings
                                                  many heads would
turn in your direction. And I wouldn't care at all, not at
all. You need it and deserve it
                                                  and I follow you with quiet
pleasure, not jealous in the least. Later, we'd talk about God
and how you lied during Confession as a girl. On our knees in
Stanley Park, we'd pray to the new emerging Power
                                                  then I'd take
you in my arms and kiss away your fears. The moonlit fog
a brightening veil from over the bay.

4.

Love can do this awful trick where you're turned
inside out and don't mind in the least.
And though walking
in the cold winter wind causes discomfort, what
with your most precious organs
exposed to the bitter freeze, buffeted about and bruised,
Love tells you it's essential for your final birth.
Then you wonder who'll love you like this—
inside out, symmetrically disgorged
with oddities hung from your casual skin
like pans from a tinker's cart.

But Love is nothing if not consistent. Though Love is also
sometimes nothing.
And there you are, standing by the river
with the icy jewelled trees of the dazzling north.
There you stand, glass-coloured globes where those
organs used to be,
the heart itself like a brilliant ruby
hanging from your chest. And the trick is
you knew all along about Love
and the reversal of fortune.
You knew better
and didn't give a tinker's damn.

Part IV

The Ghost Father

WHEN THE GHOST FATHER DIES

1.

sister called today and said you were dying for sure
this time   and would we come? you were asking for us
had heard it was someone's birthday.   not mine. and
how's she doing and ronnie—how's my son? and though
I've been preparing for this for some time   I still
had a few tears left.   the big ones the salty ones
that roll down cheeks and chin unabashed—

sweet jesus, I want you twice born in heaven   father
I want to see you once again.

HANDS

(for Robert Edgar)

it's the hands i wonder about   how may pairs before
mine with this blood   with this gene code in the knuckles?
and it's knuckles i wonder about most of all . . . for where
mine are smooth-skinned and pink   yours are wrinkled
and scarred   always swimming in grease it seemed
pulling wrenches on some bastard's cat   (never your own)
then cutting road through the cedar groves   showing
me once how the levers worked   finessing the blade
through stumps and limbs   simple shit, you said

these hands of mine have never been to war   yours scraped
steel and froze till they bleed   corvettes on the north
atlantic   oerlikons and multiple pompoms   then later
six-inchers on a cruiser . . . and hands before yours
lugging a lee-enfield through the poppies and turks   hands
skilled in ways i'll never know: ship builder, draftsman
jeweller   fingers left grasping the nightmare's cold barrel
the huns!   the bloody huns! he cried   waking in fury
long after the war . . .

tonight my hands feel useless and pale   having fluttered
through time without tools or skill   but my fingers
hit the keys with the tunes of other lives   filled
with their motion   the generous dead

THE ESSENTIAL FATHER

He wasn't an old woman, not by a long shot, and didn't dwell in anything as cozy as a shoe, no . . . but he did like his tea from time to time, and a bowl of Burley to quiet his nerves, for his peck of kids spanned diapers to teens, and he often didn't know quite what to do. Being a busy man, amateur cobbler and mystic and his time was taken up by all manner of things, especially an addiction to secret lodges. But he did try to spend lots of time with his bairns, for the biggest fix of all was his habit of fatherhood.

And had there been a fireplace in their living room, with a generous hearth and woolly rugs, he would have dozed for hours before bright blazing logs covered with children and musty books. And evening after evening they would have danced and sang through all that was magical, innocent, and full of colour . . . But there was no living room to speak of, really, just an old front porch with a brown canvas tarp that was much too cold in autumn and winter.

There were other ways to gather, however—particularly in dead of night and cold of winter—for there was an enormous bathroom with a huge marble tub that defied description . . . and how such a luxury came to be in the home of one so poor is one of the many mysteries this tale will not resolve. But it was there and hot water at the end of the day though the water ran very slowly from the taps and took forever to fill the tub . . . but there was some sagacity in this as though a deeper natural order were working in the very plumbing of the house.

Because of the volume of water needed, and the length of time in filling the giant alembic, the entire family bathed together sequentially; and for a variety of reasons it was decided that the father should enter the tub first, sitting with his back to the cool marble. He then took one child at a time starting with the youngest and smallest and as the water level rose he would chat with each child about the business of his or her day (general progress, nasty heartaches, or other forms of "ouchness").

In this fashion he was able to spend time with each of his offspring, sustaining the elemental bond and dispensing Sophia's love in the warmest and sudsiest way: all while splashing mirthfully, though occasionally knocking over the tea service that always stood ready and piping hot at his elbow. Of course as the children grew up modesty required bathing attire and the father himself took to wearing an enormous striped affair like a big yellow and blue awning. And then tub-time was like a visit to the ocean—which the family had never made due to the awkwardness of penury—but the ocean was there all the more in imagination and each child, each fruit of the father's loins, did receive a special tale from the depths of time and from around the globe.

And as the years passed, the children often wondered how the old founder kept up his inventiveness—for there were fourteen children plus assorted pets and each and every one got their very own special yarn on bath night. The secret, of course, came later long after everyone had been scrubbed clean as Patrick's tin whistle for then the old man (by now) would clean the tub carefully checking the silt that gathered by the ominous black rubber stopper.

And here the stories began, for with uncanny instinct and preternatural grace the ancient woolgatherer sifted through the atomized earth—finding here a speck from Tibet, there a mote from the Stone Age, here a macula from a distant star. And the Allness of Everything would rush about in his mind like a tempest of love, and the tales filter down from the starry clouds and slowly get ready for telling. And of these he never wrote a single one down—not wanting more than his children's well-being: including clean ears, fingers, hair and such. Stories to keep them scrubbing in the tub.

TERRORS FROM BEYOND THE GRAVE

they buried each other in turn dug holes exactly six feet
deep threw lilies where bodies would lie said prayers
consoled the living . . . they were very disciplined it was
like a science for them shovels brightly polished smooth
grained handles lightly varnished leather gloves tastefully
black but also utilitarian

yes they were a morbid bunch from grandad down to the twins
who's going first? the old gaffer ventured beauty before age!
as he turned to the woman who passed for his wife not on your
life you old bastard! then softening, she whispered in his ear
you look so nice in pastels i just can't picture you down
there in black

if i come back as a zombie i'll blend with the night he
chortled and this impressed the twins they were really
into zombies and could hardly wait to go themselves they
were sure they'd be back before dawn dribbling and slobber-
ing for human flesh even bigger terrors from beyond the grave!

GULF WAR MEDITATIONS: ST. PETER'S ABBEY

1.

January 23, 1991

One couple came to the Abbey to end their
marriage. Uncoupling will be like a long
meditation, they explained, by the weekend
we won't even be eating together! But
the war changed everything. Armageddon.
Babylon. Christ akimbo at the end of Time.
They can't wait to get into bed now, and
break all of St. Benedict's Rules in the
process. Eros over Thanatos. It's only
Thursday, yet they can both hardly walk.

Penance wore them out—
that and the crummy sagging springs.

HOW ELVIS WOULD HAVE WEPT FOR THE CHILDREN OF BAGHDAD

2.

"There is no God but God!" they scream as burnt bodies
are pulled from the bombed Baghdad bunker. Hundreds
of black corpses with tiny charred fingers. At Saint
Peter's Abbey, washing machines bang and churn next to
my room while monks trade Valentines with the guests.
One woman from up north refuses to read the poems I've
assigned, while this very instant, someone is dropping
dead in my old home town, Vancouver. I secretly hope
it's the guy who trashed my first book in the paper,
but make an effort to be kind: my Host would prefer
it. Elvis now sings,"Love Me Tender," though I brush
my teeth in a fury, grinding bristles at the thought of
those innocent children—"Only a God can save us,"
Heidegger says somewhere. "Love me true," adds Elvis.

EROTIC THOUGHTS
AS THE WORLD PREPARES FOR WAR

3.

I am still inclined to marvel at the beauty of
your face and limbs, knowing all too well their
tendency towards death. Flowers are like this,
though their passage from beauty to dust is
quicker than ours: the petals of the portulaca,
for instance. How much more, then, is your body
when anointed with loving caresses. Aureole of
hair, curling golden-russet leaves, white bark
turned to the moon's last quarter. This autumn
when you flee from my winter mind and mood,
take heart from the promise of the trillium.

EGG PERFECTION

I love you and you love me and though Stalin butchered
millions, he sprang from the egg as surely as you and I.

And what can we do about it? Pray to Jesus? He sprang
from the egg and right onto a tree: nailed, mocked, slain.

I love me and you love you and though Jesus loved the masses,
He sprang from the egg as surely as you and I—

And what's to be done about it? Nothing. For the egg
holds the cup in its white perfection.

CRYPTO EROTICA

So we don't make love anymore, who's the worse
for wear? Besides, when you finally write a book
you'll make royalties enough to float us both
across the Pacific. Aahhh, sonorous, sibilant
Gauguin—all the best words begin with 'S':
salacious, salubrious, sanguineous, sexy.

So simple satyrs samba on the seashore, and
coffee-coloured maidens lean naked over my
hammock. This is the life—even our holy
Lord might have taken His time down here
beneath gentler palms. No rush to the cross,
no frozen northern angst.

We don't make love anymore and so both dream
of light on a far blue sea. Distance raised to
virtue—illumination on the side.

TO DAPHNE WITH HER GLOVES OFF

Love, I give you one
more chance—take the
tape from my ribs,
the casts from my
fists. Love, the
swelling around my
eyes has subsided,
and the green shines
through, emerald and
fine. Love, in your
many incarnations
you have won all the
matches. But the
beatings get milder
each time.

THE MARTYRED BUGS

Leatherjackets aren't so tough, riding blithely into any place
they want—I whap them with rolled up newspapers and they
crumble, O how they crumble—their long legs kicking like June
Taylor dancers, high-stepping to the wind's brisk rhythm—then
Whap, Whap, Whap, all the joy stripped from their merry dance,
Whap! Whap! Whap! Clinging to the walls like forgotten saviours:
O God, O God, why hast Thou forsaken us? These are the aban-
doned of all bugs. Hungry for love with their Hollywood pins, they
dream of polished hardwood floors, bright footlights, crowds
of cheering army grunts. But now, smeared to a wall like Our
Lord on the cross, it freaks me out—the pathos, the pathos!
And I pray for their forgiveness—pass them vinegar on sponge
and toothpick. I divide their coriaceous garments. I even stick
pins in their sides, just to make sure—no water and wine, but
signum they are, nevertheless, broken and bent, stuck to the
paradise of my white plaster wall.

FROGS AND WASPS

Onion Lake.   Spring.   20 below.
Red ice on morning lagoon.
Country in peril.   Frogs
and wasps.   Life on the pond
is violent.   Stick to flies,
froggy   stick to butterflies.
Wasps   on the other hand,
steal favours from their royal
cousins, the bees.   They are
only good for malice and the
raping of plums.

At Onion Lake the sweet grass
grows thin and gold in winter.
The honey pond takes all
the shit we can give it.
The beavers no longer eager,
the country tired.

Part V

Stream Under Flight

STREAM UNDER FLIGHT

3.

butterflies in sunlight, moths at night. the mercury vapour lamp a siren for bugs, now stuck to the screen like petals. in the morning you sweep them down while fat spiders perch quietly on the porch. but then everything odd is beautiful: like the woman who comes to tea and to argue. her hair black silk, her heart set deep in a silver cocoon. no one tastes her luminous beauty: all her rings turned to secrets on a chain around her neck; her smiles filled with stillness, the courage of the chaste.

4.

above the caraganas a meadowlark sings, yellow blossoms dripping with rain. a young woman—stone faced—dances in the yard. never does she tire of moving her limbs, this daughter, this eldest child. even soaked to the bone, she turns from your offer of warmth. loving her so much, this is hard to get beyond, and you pray for an end to her painful doubt. but she'll find her way out, never fear—you just crush with your love and caustic tongue. every step too heavy for flight.

6.

for fifteen years you've argued with that woman. now smarter than ever, she's also thicker at waist and hips. but you, too, show your age: breathless, stout, weary from waltzing. when life comes knocking, you feign disease. but such a nice face, your dark lover croons, trying to fix your tie. so what fades faster than blossoms? you think, recalling a union long ago. a small white porch, cherry petals—gone like a dream that other wife, those first two kids. your hands still trembling, shoes untied with the memory.

11.

today, let's toast Sylvia: lips like tender wishes, hands like eager dreams. you loved her well in your own fashion, but she never shut up in bed. for years you couldn't sleep! now she's gone to the bone yard—silenced by her own sad will. when you tasted her, though, there was joy enough for two, and spasms clapped your ears and rang away the pain. today who's left to remember? a silk shirt thrown carelessly—her mouth so alive at your breast.

13.

two doors east, a woman with sable hair. once you were lovers tossing in bed. once you were friends playing at house. now you're apart and share the same joke. yet morning till dusk you trade stones and aspersions: "get your dog shit off my lawn!"; "get your grass off my dog's shit!" back and forth like myna birds, the laughter's infectious—so you'd think. but not many see the depth of this love, and the locals say you're mad. two old shoes crossing a stream.

14.

out here you're "professor". in the shadow of garbage mountain, you almost pass for a prominent man. but in the city—behind your back—they call you bum, uncouth, a man of fetters. who lives well in the eyes of others? who goes far without tripping a few times? not everyone with a hat can get ahead in this world. forget the predators, remember the lamb. or better yet, those black cows grazing. the gold stubble rising to meet their patient lips.

22.

by the old town hall, a sheen of roses. palominos at sunset like something other, tails and manes now candles aflame. but these mares—fair maidens in thick green grass—only have eyes for ribbons and boys. so you circle the field with a metal detector, lost change going for coffee or beer. and silence fills dusk like water from a stream, your mind becoming a cup.

25.

Fritz Perls couldn't do it out Cowichan Valley—not Jung on a scroll or Bubba Ram Das. acid didn't do it or magic morels. not love, lust, or a blend of both: sweet lips and fingers on a carousal of flesh. no words come close, though poems come near: sunlight falling through a stand of red cedar, dust motes dancing by heavy green boughs. silence a way, but never the goal. it calls even now—this stream under flight.

28.

your shack's on the edge of a working field, but you don't work the garden much anymore. a few herbs and onions, a hill of spuds. the rest gone to hell and purple loosestrife. Meanwhile—on the highway south—crows feast daily on some poor creature's fate. is man just a crow with occasional manners? appetite is appetite: beaks and teeth. yet how quiet you've become amidst elms and spruce, muttering over a bowl of cold rice, slumbering with pen and empty paper. maybe there is a way: the rise and fall of a single breath; the end of a line where vision blossoms.

30.

clothes and belly fit only for the sticks, you shun Broadway lights and the chic West End. besides, who goes to tailors these days? though your father and the loggers dressed well in the forties. so, no sharp crease or pleats in your pants—no classy fabric to breathe in and out. just cheap stretchy stuff dusty and worn. Szumigalski in the pocket of your coat full of holes; Han Shan stuffed deep in an old leather bag. a few bucks for the road and look who's under way—ball cap adorned with wings and fins.

36.

hopping through branches out front, that crow never strays too far from the trunk. once he might have carried books—the *tao te ching*, for example, or the *diamond sutra*—but now he's lost more than he ever learned. hungry, he eats; tired, he sleeps. who can match the sparkle in his ancient eye? who would ever think that his forked tongue would heal?

39.

on that road to the city, people rush off to work. just east of town, you can hear them cursing. yes, once you envied the fruits of their labour: big office, big car, big money. but now you've got your own work, and your hands are never still. in spring a garden for potatoes and herbs—in winter you dig snow and scatter seed for the birds. who needs a briefcase for gathering wood? deep within a breath you find real wages, while nothing of value shows up on the market. try tao jones for a lasting return.

46.

let's drop all this crap about who knows what—when the lord's coming back, who's damned or saved. why not just agree that the mystery's getting deeper? that wise folks sleep well knowing nothing at all. so tend to your carrots and columbine; learn to brew tea, be kind to kids. the breath rises and falls like a ship at sea. the mind unfurled—well into the stream.

47.

they talk of a tree older than words, back to the days when this was all bush, roots curling down to an ancient seabed. speechless, it's been called the bole of truth—in stillness it's listened to a hundred different tongues. now most only see that blackened bark, the lightning scars of its riven trunk. but its aged core is a diamond grain; free of attention, it's rooted in flight.

54.

doing everything you were told—mastering the art of pleasing others—look where you've landed. this drafty shack in a cold hard land, no leaves on the trees six months of the year. and that honking last night, that drunken wake: geese flying south with all the ponds frozen. so why waste the time left in your flask? take a cue from that field across the path. in august it blooms green and yellow—but in winter it's quiet with nothing in mind.

56.

magpies outside the door at dawn, though old storm windows deaden their chatter. music in your eyes as red berries sparkle; branches full of waxwings eating their fill; that slender pink rowan arousing winter. who deserves these hues around your house? who'd think so little could be so so much? your eyes see thrones wherever they rest.

62.

on the edge of this field, you could write a good story with only
four words. it would open and close with,
"I am not here".

64.

if you're looking for a spot to rest your mind, forget the Rockies or those western isles. tourists flock there like gulls at a dump, and the clink of silver is louder than hell. why not seek the humblest place—buy a hut and sit still on the edge of a field. no one eats better than the coyotes and crows. and all year long birds visit from afar: goldfinches, orioles, meadowlarks, geese. even lofty pelicans heading up north. after years of handshakes—the honesty of wings.

67.

in winter the snow is a provisional sea: water over earth, air over water, fire in the sky, in the fieldstone hearth. who cares if the snowplough's sometimes late? you're not going anywhere in the world that matters. porridge on the shelf and water in the tank; enough wood for months to heat your house. so let cold roads vanish and bright ways open. dwelling in quiet—a living stone in the stream.

70.

from atop trash mountain the prairie falls away: light snow and stubble, thickets of willow, birch, aspen, manitoba maple. at your feet a long lake full of trout and pike. to the north a small city of gamy passions. then tiny hamlets west and south, with bright painted shacks for old folks and bums. dawn lends its light: saffron and rose. just breathe with your eyes whenever you can.

76.

you'd give a monk the shirt off your back, and a drunk your last bowl of rice. why get stuck on the things of this world when the only way out's through the eye of a . . . noodle? life is a gift so pass it around—and don't sit doodling till your skull's in the weeds: no one gets more than the giver. harbingers of death, these stingy hearts. barren lives on the banks of the stream.

77.

so many friends gone, old and young: all under ground with no need for breath. but dawn hits the rime and a world explodes, light pointillistic falling from trees. and that shadow with hat just out past the elms? an old trucker with dog trying to heal, his hours all stolen by nameless fear. but now silence, the field, gathers him in, tears quickly turning to pins of brightness. no answers, no words, no two cents' worth—just a turn in the mind, this stream under flight.

Part VI

New Poems

A WOMAN DREAMS

1.

a woman dreams about yellow and slowly her world becomes lemons, buttercups, and rooms facing east to catch the genial morning light.

slowly her life becomes a singular event—or more to the point—a stream of such events. she's always okay when alone; she's always okay when not married.

but how many years with one man then another? the last taking up more than a decade, which is a very long time to look at all the wrong colours.

2.

a woman dreams about horses then decides to leave her second marriage. all night she rides over high mountain passes, then plods through the day arguing and weeping.

after twelve years crying, she has had enough. many believe her husband is demented—even dangerous—and though unsure of this harsh view, she admits he's been depressed most of his life.

what to do? what to do? she's worried herself to sleep for years. *if I leave he will surely die,* she ponders, for that's how huge this poor woman's heart really is. big enough to stall the death of a madman.

3.

a woman dreams about yellow, then wakes up fresh and says, *why don't you dream about yellow, too?* so the man tries hard as he can and sleeps on yellow sheets, puts lemon in his tea, and even rings his bed with yellow tulips and carnations.

but nothing works. there is a chemical missing in his brain—a simple enzyme, so to speak, controlling the enjoyment of all things yellow.

without it the man cannot smile, talk cheerfully to dogs, or keep wives in his bed for any length of time. he's not entirely selfish, however, and sees the havoc he wreaks in other lives. but what can he do, live alone? *yes*, he thinks, *yes, to avoid battles.*

4.

the man dreams about living alone after losing his second wife. she dreamt about horses and rode off into an early morning light. in the dawn, she wore a large white stetson capped with yellow rosebuds.

she sang quietly to herself in a funny croaking voice. *beauty is in the ear of the beholder*, she warbled, and never once looked back.

left alone, the man stopped dreaming altogether, and spent all his time searching the horizon. it was too painful to look at things close-up.

5.

the house he lived in was awash with mementos of their time together: furniture, drapes, dishes, pictures, their son. all tokens of her kindness, *which was like bread from god,* he thought, for she had given him a home for more than a decade.

but his disease had also filled her years with weeping. *someday,* she had feared, *all my tears will fill this house like an aquarium, and I will become either a fish or a drowned corpse.*

this was long before she dreamt of horses or of the colour yellow. but she knew in her heart that she could not become a fish. she prayed to jesus, and even he had to admit that she wasn't fish stock. *it's just not in the cards for you,* he said to her one night while wiping tears from her eyes, *have you ever thought of . . .*

6.

jesus was about to give her some sterling advice when he was called away on another line. *just hang on a sec, will ya?* he beseeched her, but then never got back at all. *was it a faulty connection*? she later mused. had she failed to pay some debt, or were the phone lines down in heaven?

she waited a long time with the receiver in the crook of her slender neck, but eventually—when her shoulder began to ache—she had to break the connection. she never held it against jesus, but could not take him seriously for years—until he'd asked for her pardon by sending a single yellow rose.

7.

thank heavens for pills, they both said together one day, for the man had gone to a doctor—on the advice of his ex-wife—who prescribed a new anti-depressant. so he took the drug faithfully for a year, and heavens what a change. he now dreamt of yellow on a regular basis, wore soft orange and lemony sweaters, and dyed all his t-shirts citrus colours.

it wasn't enough to bring the woman back from her flight through the mountains, but he felt hope stirring in the grey mists of his soul. perhaps horses would appear in his dreams. perhaps he too would journey to the top of the world, looking down on towns like revelstoke and golden.

by the time he got to kamloops, however, his horse would be very tired, for the man was large boned and heavy: like an argument for the existence of god. *if you allow that creation is an ontological mystery,* the horse would say at parting, *then mystery subsumes all rational attempts to analytically encompass it.* this seemed like good sense—even in imagination—and the man stood waiting for his dream horse, waiting to ride.

8.

one morning the woman phoned the man as he sat in the kitchen having tea; she said that she'd dreamt about him the night before: *we were down on the farm*, she said, *and you were dressed in raggedy old underwear that was falling off your bum. somehow the house was on the edge of a precipice and water was swirling all around, eating away at the earth and threatening to throw us over the edge. you were diving into deep streams and swimming gracefully, like a dolphin through very clear water. climbing out then diving in, over and over again.*

then later in the dream, she mumbled trying to light a small cigar, *I was in mexico with friends. you were there, too, and one fine day we joined Andrew Lloyd Webber beside a pool. he knew you already and was teasing you about something or other. I whispered in your ear, "just don't lose your temper—besides, you're a bigger man than he."*

that's quite a dream, the man replied, not knowing where to look anymore or where to put his hands. then he picked up the cat, thistle, and stroked her quickly till she purred with satisfaction. *Andrew Lloyd Webber be damned,* he muttered and smiled.

but he liked the dolphin part, and realized that he was never meant to ride off on a horse wearing yellow sports apparel. he was first and foremost a creature of water: a mendicant diver in ragged-ass shorts swimming close to the edge of another's peril. *perhaps I am a peril diver,* he sniggered, too pleased with himself—as usual. *laugh when you can? it never hurts.*

9.

when the walls arose, the woman became a total stranger, though he knew every pore of her body, every beauty mark and blemish. also, her hair became longer, more lustrous, like jet-black silk or satin. *rapunzel in a tower, awaiting a hero to climb down to.*

she denied it, of course: *I am heloise, forever! and you? you are my beloved abelard.* but he saw horses grazing beneath the fall of her hair, and knew someone soon would ride from afar. a crown of lemon blossoms to wake the day.

ELEGY FOR ANOTHER LOST BOY

1.

your words are best when you don't speak them.
your chest, for example, is covered with stories
too private to ever be published. they are
exquisite, too, like the skulls of small
children drowned at sea.

but words are, finally, too great a temptation,
implying as they do communion—
for you, another face is always an
excuse for deception.

another face, another pair of eyes and ears.
you must always put what you think
is your best foot forward. though it is
an ugly thing, your *best* foot.

twisted almost beyond recognition, what first
appear to be toes are leeches
set by your mother on those childhood feet.
this will keep you from running away.

2.

and so you put your foot forward, cheerfully
even boldly at times, but no one
in the crowd is deceived.

and when the race begins, you crouch on
the starting line with everyone else.
you chatter more than anyone
about the thrill and value
of manly competition.

and where others wear sturdy track shoes
made of the finest leather, your
misshapen extremities
are wrapped in sacks.

when the starting pistol is raised
into the air, you seem feverish,
almost ecstatic to be with people
in the clear spring air. yes, there
on the grass beneath a vault
of deepening blue.

3.

for a moment before the blast of the gun
you look around, and everything
has been drawn up into an exalted
condition—stillness and dignity falling
over every surface attractive to light.

and when the report comes, the others speed
off to the west faster than any mortals
you've ever seen. and they never look back—

yes, they will claim their bright medals when
across the finish line, as you hobble in circles,
retying your jute sacks in the glorious sun.
as you sing your mother's favourite hymn:
everything comes to those who wait.

THE SECRET NAME

their son dead at the age of five and this
world stands still for those who love them.
I don't know what to say—a common refrain
among friends gathering on the phone lines.
and we are speechless in the midst of our

late winter days—stand still, struck dumb,
while owen goes to sleep, rocking in his
father's arms. and in toronto there is no
sound of any kind: no wind, no sirens, no
squabbling cabbies or beggars in boxes
and blankets. there is only a cold quiet
brightness, crueller by far than the darkness
we sleep in. and yes, the betting

machines are silent in bigliardi's off yonge
street. the baritones of brag are suddenly
mute with their unlit stogies. and on small
screens, horses in florida are frozen in
motion. not racing now, they too are intent
only on listening—for a small soul passing

and silence our prayer. the boy's secret
name laid in rose oil and linen. who can
fathom this passage? who will
name this loss?

BROADWAY BENEDICTION

1.

sometimes hanging on by our fingers for the
sake of the boy we know it's wrong—that it's
never worked for anyone else. we climb stairs
up and down the house to avoid one another,
though I find your sable hair everywhere. I
don't know what a woman tastes like anymore
while you fancy stallions of silver and jade.

what's missing? we are not without love, you say,
not without a kind of communion, and I agree.
at the end of a world, at the edge of this place
of plants and other dreams, I want only you
beside me. the voice that completes my own.

but though I find jet-black webs on my coat,
there's a scent in the air of burning leaves and
branches—raspberry stalks fruitless and dried
withering in the flames—while a small dog runs
circles in the yard, his name forgotten. where
does one pursue the highest form of love?

2.

yes, today I walk streets wet from last night's
rain and bars welcome me, pals hang out doors
with cigars and brown pints. there is talk of books
and words—ideas flow from mouth to ear—while
a cool drizzle returns and windows fog with time,
with the mirth of old friends. this flush of words
like a drifting narcotic haze.

we think we are thinking, think we are speaking,
polish our nails against worn lapels. but secretly
in dark and deep—where something beats like a
heart—there is a winnowing of spirit, words falling
like yesterday's yellow chaff, ideas shocked and
stooked. and what to do after all but tenderly
touch an arm, ruffle a head of flaxen hair, brush
a cheek with dry lips.

3.

a man's wife has died a painful death but no words come to mind, no fair phrases from catechisms and catacombs. I take his hot hands in lieu of speech, search his eyes, then suddenly recall the shimmer of mercury under glass in summer starlight. *spirit is that which loves and knows* I whisper, and brightly—as if grounded by a mirror—the figure of a woman steps lightly over a lucid sill.

4.

leaving the bar, heading back home, I stop to buy
news from an old street vender. and though a big
man, his voice is like a penny whistle, tooting
childlike and cheerful about anything you want.
being an outcast, his words take the shape of a
small begging bowl. but in the eyes of the poor
are the sharpest reflections.

what he says is this: *worked all morning in a
garden out of town, and boy am I tired. selling
papers is nothing compared to weeding!* but what
I see in his eyes are two shallow tins, with light
from invisible tapers. *mirrors always more than
they seem,* I think, passing him a coin.

5.

crossing the street at a butcher's, I see windows
full of lamb chops and wild boar. friends meanwhile—
in a coffee house—wave, crunch pastries,
sip coffee. but their hunger's not mine as I pass a
piano store on the corner; ebony reflected in plate
glass windows, and I'm caught. the soul wells up
glimmering like water crowned by sun—
Helios, a threshold, lucid and still

then wildly bright! this roaring confluence! as I
hang fast to parking meters while furious floods
tug my mind. *rivers always more than a stream,*
I think. this flow in every direction becoming lake
small sea then inland ocean. with dolphins riding
the liminal waves like wingless angels.

even standing by a rickety old movie house, I
stream all over town: the mind totally backlit
as if dancing brightly on pelagic truths known
but never spoken. and maybe I'll grab a bite
after all, though no hunger remains. maybe I
will throw an arm around a mate, grind seeds
for words, knead flour for cakes and commiseration:
in short, prepare a light feast.

6.

and what's there to do amidst all this jazz? like
stroke a face tenderly, with soothing sounds we
all agree make sense; or look deeply into the eyes
of someone you love. and why not? death passes
lightly over this threshold of hope—a *solificatio,*
the crowning light—a sight worth seeing.

then another raven hair on my rough woollen
sleeve. ever mindful, should I lose myself, you've
thrown me a line without words or conditions.
and as the flood recedes, I turn lovingly to one
at the edge of my world. whose voice, without
knowing, completes my own. holding by our
fingertips to what we know.

EPI/LOGOS

1.

poets in the living room for hours this afternoon
all ages, sizes, sexes—though I guess there's only
two of the latter. but many proclivities, right?
nod, wink, nod, wink! with so many orifices
to choose from, and so many appendages to
lubricate and buff in the buff.

I, for example, am a man of the tongue, and my
tongue is both business and pleasure for I dream
of a woman with a clit in her ear: I want my poems
to send her rocking; I want to whisper *l'amor, luna,*
liquorice, luminescent or *I luff you baby, I want to*
luff you so bad. . .

like bringing her bow into the wind is so wild, and
she'll thank me for it later as we ride the gentle
waves in harbour; grappling gently with iron hooks,
sending salvos of hard love through each other's
rigging—but fuck this nautical shit!

2.

I'm getting seasick for sure, wanting *love* not *luff,*
and can't spell worth a cosmic shit when excited by
the presence of several erotically charged minds—
l'amor, luna, luminescent, I whisper into the dusty
air, the wintry motes all dry and charged—almost
like antimatter—while ice crystals lift off the snow
in a fog; *like jesus with bigger hands reaching* to
that hard orange sun, that candid luminescence.

then spreading it over our cold callous earth, like
a comforter of love; and jesus wants me to luff him
too, quietly turns me into the wind and drops anchor
alongside, taming the fire in my head, in my hold.
this ship of the poetic line always blown between
fire and water.

3

but it's simply what's given at forty below zero, in
this frozen limbo of jive-assed poetasters; where
nothing waves except the memory of wheat, and
nothing harbours except a grudge, while the tide
out here is only detergent—and will I die without
seeing my salt spring island grave?

but jesus just blows gently into my sails and says,
the seas are bigger than you've ever known, so don't
worry about your spelling. which I don't, looking
hungrily at those ears and thinking one more time

rock on, sweet baby, rock on my tongue like flame
from seraphic lips, my heart all sticky like a liquorice
moon. *l'amor, luminescence* I whisper, then make
like a song for open water.

BENEATH THE HEART VIBRATING TO WORDS

1.

Duncan is young but not small He is fat and soft like a pillow and one might say he is all foam that he carries no muscle at all But his deep green eyes are not soft They are brilliant like emeralds and speak of vast dreams and a wily intelligence

When he runs to the school grounds they are usually empty and the soft green fields stretch around the old wooden buildings to the foot of the hills Does he notice the flowers beneath the classroom windows?

I think not but he loves the dandelions and pulls them out of the ground saving as much stem as he can Pretty bouquets for his aunty or maybe the red-haired girl whose grandpa owns the big department store

I call him to me *duncan* I say *let's play catch* and he laughs and bounces over to a small diamond laid out in the shadow of tall cedars and fir After when he's winded and sweaty I feed him grapes oranges slices of apple *no more starches* I say after one small banana Will he ever lose weight?

I can only imagine the teasing he endures But he likes to eat and finds simple comfort in the very worst things white bread and cheese spread chocolate chip cookies If only I knew where he got such trash There's usually only the two of us and I follow the strictest diets

Tender soft gentle quiet His huge green eyes absorb the fields of summer and I never want to lose him never want him to grow up That's silly of course but let me enjoy these fleeting years that seem like afternoons

Yes he is foam soft like a pillow yet inside there is a measure of rawhide something tough to take on a world if need be When he walks to church on sunday through town and up the wooded lane people stop and watch him pass *there is more to him than meets the eye* someone whispers Rawhide for ropes and reins emerald eyes for crossing over

2.

Dusk has fallen and we're walking home when down the hill comes a brute of a boy Leather jacket and thick boots unfiltered cigarettes in his tee-shirt pocket Duncan seems to know him and moves off the walk with a nervous shudder *don't worry* I say *he won't touch you when I'm around*

But then I'm not always around Long days when the boy must make his way alone through town The toughs outside the pool hall or cruising the streets in their old jalopies

In the ripe cherry light this one seems covered with tiny rubies pimples not come to a head *hey fatty* he says to my boy *what's the matter you still scared I'm gonna steal your lunch?* Outrageous as if I'm not even present There's no respect for anything these days

But duncan just smiles and takes my hand At least this time it's nothing worse than words and what are they compared to this summer evening

The smell of fresh cut grass the tangy scent of cedars drooping over the fence with its lilac garland Tomorrow we'll pick berries in matsqui the fields full of butterflies white on red and green

3.

Downtown at twilight and we're walking to the movies to see a scary flick *Frankenstein's Daughter* it's called and duncan's got a comic to hide behind But passing the tracks we see the poor kids playing with nothing

Sticks and stones flying through the air taunts and curses to make me blush So much anger this early in life Will they all become monsters for real? holy terrors in blue shorts and dirty runners?

But then someone calls out *zorro I'm zorro* and everything changes One last game before heading home those small welfare houses on the crest of the hill A tall thin boy with black hair slices the air with his stick and Z's appear everywhere the light allows Under street lamps and neon signs in the flashing bright cones from passing cars

This tale demands elegance from everyone involved *hey dunkey* they shout *come over and be sergeant garcia we're all too skinny*

Duncan giggles not offended in the least these tough kids take their share of beatings *maybe tomorrow* he calls back *if I'm not picking berries* I'll make sure he goes I think to myself for there's nothing sweeter than the sharing of dreams Even play can lead to heaven

4.

We all gather in yards on porches and even dogs leave off chasing cats when the shadow appears in the midst of day Downtown in the hatchery the hens start to huddle by their favourite roost Duncan and the other kids have been given boxes with special holes for a solar eclipse is not something to be seen directly

We cross the schoolyard to stand by second base on our favourite diamond *which hole do I look in?* the boy asks but then accidentally crushes the cardboard contraption *don't worry* I reply *we'll watch it from the safety of our minds*

Closing our eyes as the field darkens here on pine street the crowd is looking through beer bottles exposed film anything that shields the orbs It is not a small thing when one god covers another so I look down to make sure duncan's eyes are closed

His navy gym shorts are pulled high over his belly his striped tee-shirt tucked in all red white and blue A small boy wrapped in a flag I think as we stand at attention Everywhere in town there is stillness and quiet

Greasers by the legion have put down their fists farmers in matsqui stand by their tractors half finished smokes crushed on the ground Abbotsford is breathless those chestnut trees by the rink glowing luminous green from the sun's corona Even duncan glows His face like a mirror coming out of the mist

John Livingstone Clark is the author of *Prayers and Other Unfinished Letters*, *Passage to Indigo*, *Stream Under Flight*, *Stepping Up to the Station*, *Breakfast of the Magi*, *Back to Bethany: Eighty-nine Paragraphs about Jesus and Lazarus in Abbotsford*. The poems in this Selected are from these volumes.

John Livingstone Clark lives in Saskatchewan.